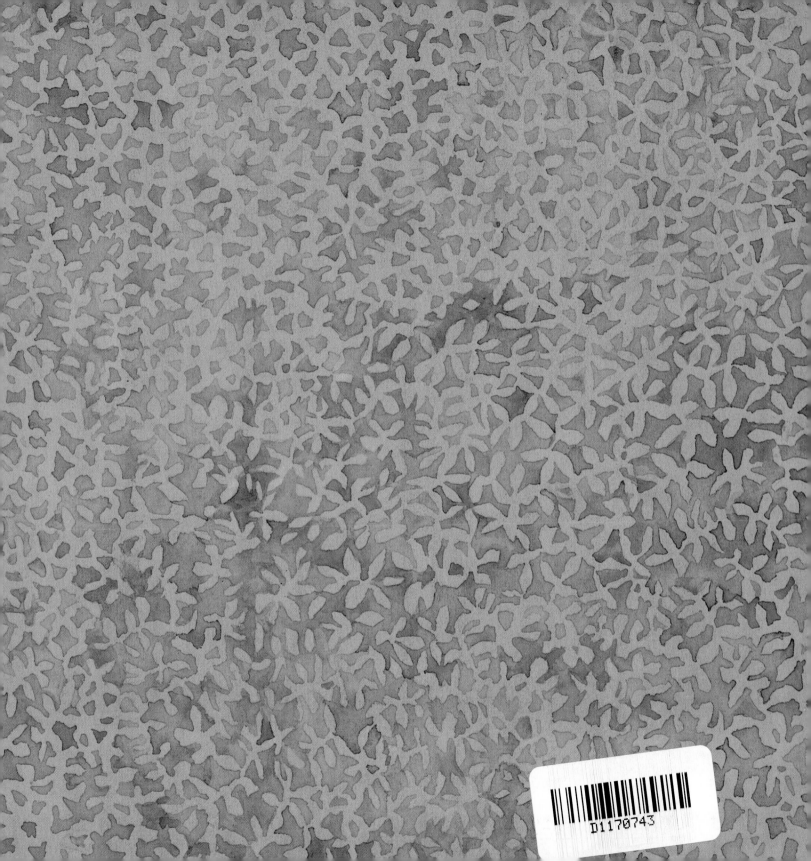

Scripture taken from the HOLY BIBLE, NEW INTERNATIONAL READER'S VERSION™,
Copyright © 1995, 1996, 1998 by International Bible Society. Used by permission of
Zondervan Publishing House. All rights reserved.

Printed in U.S.A.
ISBN  0-8054-2167-X

**Library of Congress Cataloging-in-Publication Data**

Eckard, Leslie.
  Which came first, the chicken or the egg? / by Leslie Eckard ; illustrations by Judy Sakaguchi.
      p. cm.
  ISBN 0-8054-2167-X
  1. God--Juvenile literature. 2. Creation--Juvenile literature. [1. God. 2. Creation.] I.
Sakaguchi, Judy, ill. II. Title.

  BT107 .E32 2001
  231--dc21

                                                                              00-049808

1 2 3 4 5   05 04 03 02 01

# Which Came First, the Chicken or the Egg?

• Written by Leslie Eckard • Illustrated by Judy Sakaguchi •

BROADMAN
&HOLMAN
PUBLISHERS

Which came first,
the chicken
or the egg?

3

4

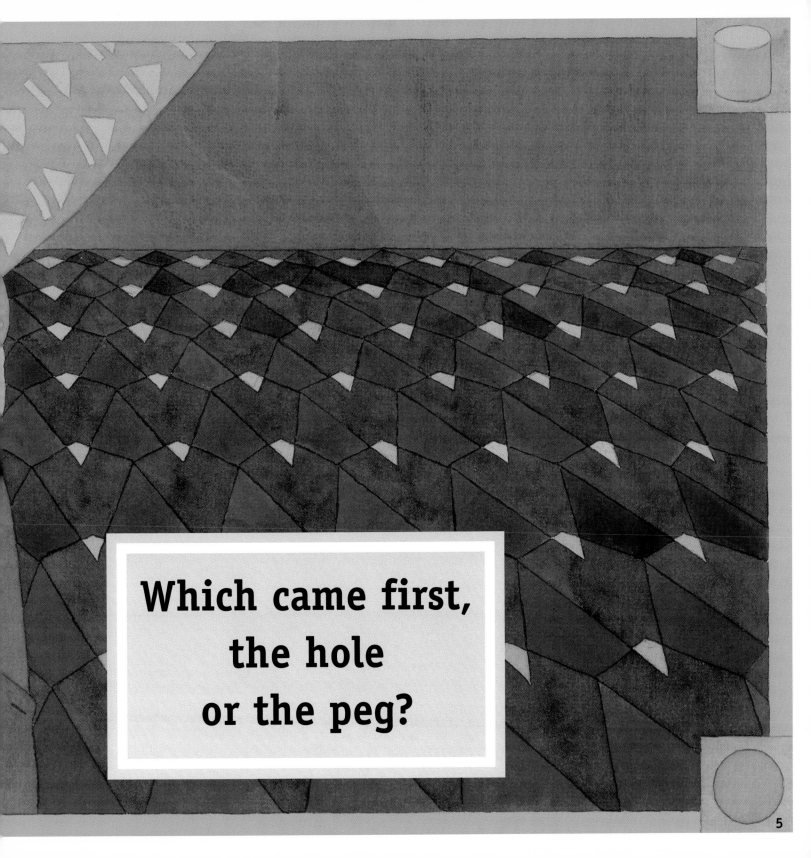

**Which came first,
the hole
or the peg?**

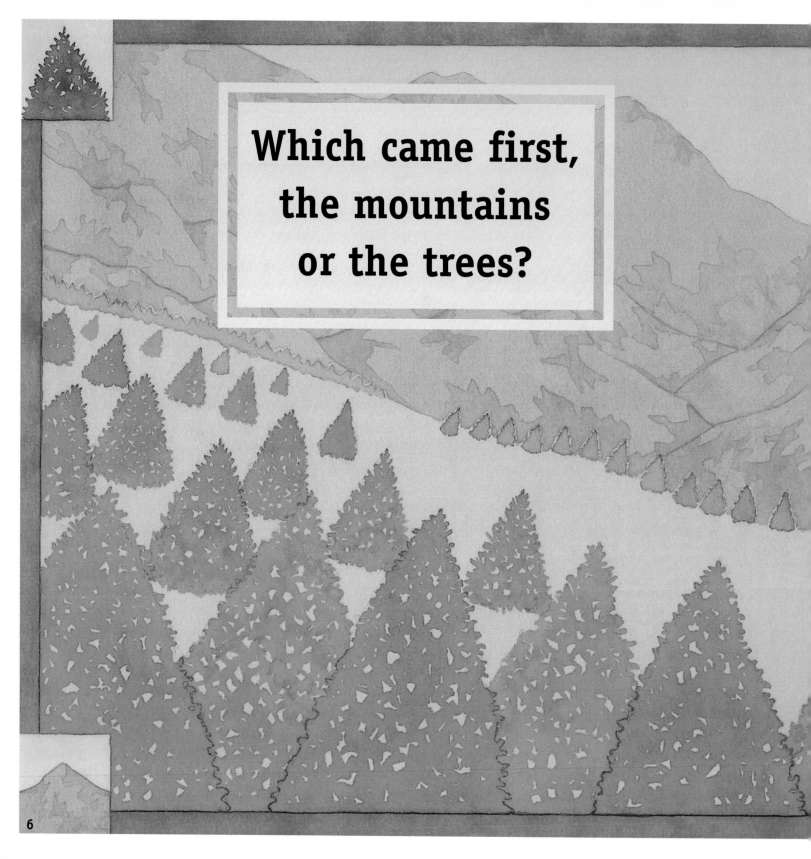

**Which came first,
the mountains
or the trees?**

**Which came first, the flowers or the bees?**

9

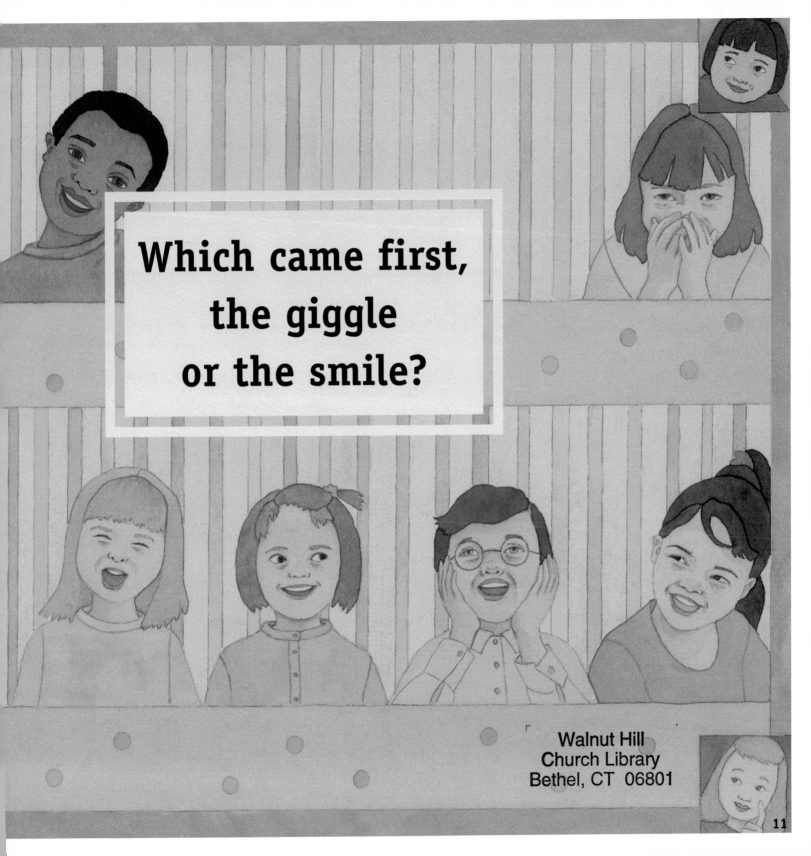

Which came first,
the giggle
or the smile?

11

**Which came first,
the inch
or the mile?**

Which came first,
the strong
or the weak?

Which came first,
the "hide"
or the "seek"?

16

**Which came first,
the stars
or the sky?**

The answer's easy,
so plain to see—
God came first,
before you and me.

God made everything
work just right,
whether night follows day,
or day follows night.

23

He made the world
and all the rest!
And when God is first,
we all are blessed.

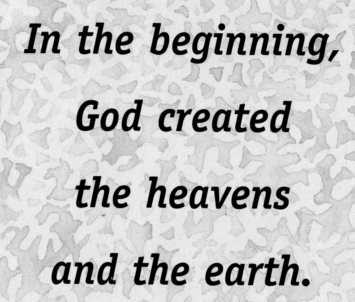

# In the beginning, God created the heavens and the earth.

## Genesis 1:1

---

Read the entire story of creation
in the first chapter of Genesis in the
*Read to Me Bible for Kids NIrV,*
from Holman Bible Publishers.